COFFEE

*The Connoisseur's
Companion*

COFFEE

*The Connoisseur's
Companion*

Cover: 15th century miniature,
Florentine school.

First published in Great Britain in 1999 by
PAVILION BOOKS LIMITED
London House, Great Eastern Wharf
Parkgate Road, London SW11 4NQ

Copyright © 1995 Nardini Editore, Fiesole (FI), Italy
Text by Daniele Rava
English translation © Pavilion Books Limited 1999

A CIP catalogue record for this book is available
from the British Library.

ISBN 1 86205 329 4

Set in Times New Roman
Printed in Italy

2 4 6 8 10 9 7 5 3 1

This book can be ordered direct from the publisher.
Please contact the Marketing Department.
But try your bookshop first.

AN ANCIENT
TRADITION

Coffee: always a friend

Rarely has the history of mankind been so closely identified with a drink as it has with coffee. Perhaps tea is the only other drink that has been known to assume an importance to some extent comparable with that of coffee, at least in some periods of its long history. Noone can ignore the fact that every morning, every time the sun rises above the horizon in any part of the world, men and women of every position bring a cup of coffee to their lips and, noisily or silently, according to the customs observed in each of the various countries, sip the hot, black, fragrant liquid.

There are of course many different ways of preparing coffee. The Arabic is perhaps the oldest. Then there are the Turkish and Greek methods, which consist of mixing together ground coffee and sugar (for those who like their coffee sweet) with water in an *ibrik*, a container with a narrow mouth and a long handle, in which the grounds rise to the surface when it boils. This is heated on the hot stove; twice the grounds must rise to the mouth of the container and twice they must be allowed to fall back again. Only then is the coffee ready to be poured, thick and boiling, into tiny cups without handles.

There is the age-old Neapolitan method in which the coffeepot is inverted when the water is hot, so that it filters through the ground coffee that has been put in the special perforated container. The coffee drips from this, a thick, full liquid rich in aromas which fire the brain into action as soon as they are smelt. Then there is the American method, in which the ground coffee and hot water are put in a glass container, usually globe-shaped, from which the steaming black drink is poured into cups that are often large.

There are the Scandinavian and Anglo-Saxon methods, where the resulting drink is not so much black as dark brown, a phenomenon caused by the beans being roasted differently. There are Indian and Indonesian methods, using milk and cream. Overall, there are almost as many methods as there are different peoples. Perhaps only the Chinese and the Japanese did not feel the need for a cup of strong coffee to wake them up in the morning. They have

always put the greatest faith in tea, very weak, made with a few leaves in suspension in the boiling water.

Certainly the Indian soldiers who served with the English in the Second World War understood the difference between coffee (which is capable of reviving strength and sensation), and tea to which so much powdered milk had been added that it formed a mixture of which it was said, "You could stand a spoon up in it". The custom of tea drinking shares the advantage with coffee that the lighter-coloured drink also contains caffeine, the extraordinary substance that, to exaggerate a little, has much of the effect of a potent drug.

It is interesting to see the rapid way that coffee is prepared in Italy: the faces

of the customers and the barman are almost concealed by the steam from the coffee machine, while the attentive eye of the customer watches the drops systematically falling into the cup, his or her mouth watering in anticipation.

Naturally, there are some who like it *macchiato* (with a dash of milk), some straight (*corretto*), some stronger (*alto*), some weaker (*ristretto*), but coffee is always dense, fragrant and hot, descending to the stomach to awaken latent moods. Its effect is quickly felt by the nerves and the brain; the new day opens with a smile; people willingly exchange words with their neighbours on the bus; they become more tolerant, more active, and readier to receive the daily instructions for what needs to be done. It may be that nobody says it, because we consider ourselves independent and free, but we feel better disposed towards other people, readier to accept even thankless tasks, in the certain hope that in a couple of hours, down at the bar or at the coffee machine in the corridor, we can sip another coffee, the better to continue the day.

Housewives have a coffee in the kitchen before starting the daily chores; employees get off the bus and run to the café; rail commuters may pause for a moment by the platform and have a coffee to warm the stomach on a cold winter's morning; farm workers drink their first coffee while the bacon is still sizzling on the fire for breakfast at dawn; and typists put their red lips to the white edge of the cup, with the little finger held upwards in a dignified manner. The ritual is completed.

An old Arab proverb says that coffee must be sipped "as hot as hell, as black as ink, as sweet as love". The Arabs have an ancient wisdom which comes to them from traditions rooted in the ancient civilisations of Mesopotamia and Egypt. Even in ancient times they realised that coffee contains substances that are stimulants, and it was probably then used more as a medicament than a habitual drink. We in the western world are not without stereotyped views, and we see coffee as the traditional drink offered by sheikhs and Moslem religious leaders to their guests in their Bedouin tents. But the traditional drink of eastern peoples almost everywhere was, in fact, tea.

What does coffee contain?

Coffee acts as a stimulant of cerebral activity; it encourages the association of ideas and helps concentration, as well as making intellectual attention more profitable; it sparks the imagination, accelerating the development of ideas and opinions, it improves eloquence, acts as a tonic, it reduces the sense of

tiredness, and it stimulates muscle tone. At least, these are all things which medical experts and researchers have said at one time or another, adding that it can also keep one awake at night.

But what is it that causes these effects? Each coffee bean contains an average of 10 per cent water, a similar

quantity of nitrogenous substances, about 10 per cent fats and sugars, 24 per cent cellulose, 1.8 per cent tannic acid, traces of volatile oils, ash, and, finally, caffeine, a substance which is part of the group of xanthines (like theobromine of cocoa and theine in tea).

Baldly described, it is a substance which exerts an exciting and stimulating action on the nervous, cardiac, muscular and sensory systems. It also has a dilating effect on the blood vessels of the brain, leading to a greater flow of blood and more oxygenation. Every 100 grams of roasted coffee contains from 1 to 3 grams of caffeine; the percentage varies a little according to the source and type, for instance Moka, Java, Santos, Costa Rica, Ceylon, and so on. With the addition of hot water about 1.8 per cent of the caffeine in the coffee grounds is extracted, so each small cup of coffee will contain from 50 to 150 milligrams of caffeine. A practical example will be more easily understood by coffee drinkers. Using a Neapolitan coffee maker (the one which is turned upside down when the water comes to the boil), a cup will contain about 150 milligrams of caffeine, while an espresso made by a professional machine will contain about 80 milligrams. So it can be seen that the coffee from the café or bar is rather healthier, even though some think it is less tasty, than that made in the house by one of the traditional methods.

Caffeine

The presence of this alkaloid in an infusion made from coffee beans is said to have first been discovered by Friedlieb Runge in 1820, but a little later it was also isolated by other scientists. There is indeed still some disagreement as to who it was who actually discovered caffeine. Various chemists, including Robiquet, Pellettier, Caventou, Mulder and, much later, Jobst, devoted themselves to achieving this. At the same time or a few years later, it was determined that the theine present in the infusion of the leaves of the tea plant had the same composition as caffeine, $C_8H_{10}N_4O_2$. The credit for this goes to Oudry, Günther and other researchers.

Caffeine, an alkaloid of the purine group, is a colourless solid, soluble in water and alcohol, which melts at 217° C (423° F). As well as being found in infusions of coffee and tea, it is present in fruits of *Paullinia sorbilis*, a plant which grows naturally in the

forests of South America. There, its black seeds are roasted and ground by the Indians to make *guaranà*, a drug used for neuralgia and migraine. It is also found in cola nuts (*Cola acuminata*) which, like the cocoa tree, belongs to the *Sterculiaceae* family. The cola nut was unknown to Europeans until 1830, but its properties were recognised by many of the Africans, who chewed the seeds for their stimulant effect. Today the cola nut is used medicinally in digestive preparations, and it is also one of the components of the best known stimulating and restorative aerated drinks.

To make caffeine for therapeutic use, the coffee is treated with steam and then with highly volatile solvents, such as benzene and dichloromethane. When the solvent has dissolved the caffeine is

removed. The coffee residue can be roasted and also used for food purposes.

Each to his own coffee

People will never tire of declaring that excessive coffee consumption can only be harmful. On the other hand, if any irritating or worrying symptoms should occur, the cure is simply to suspend or reduce the consumption of coffee. The symptoms will quickly go away.

Everyone has their own tolerance threshold to coffee, as with wine and alcohol in general. There are those who are convinced that they sleep better if they drink a coffee before going to bed, while to the depressed coffee may bring only insomnia and melancholy.

With some individuals coffee has beneficial digestive effects, but with others it may cause a tiresome burning sensation in the stomach. It increases the gastric secretion of hydrochloric acid, so anyone with gastro-duodenal ulcers must avoid drinking it, as must those with colitis, because coffee accentuates intestinal peristalsis, increasing spasms while provoking constipation.

The digestive effect is actually only valid for people suffering hypochlorhydria. If others claim to find it helpful gor digestion, the reason is that they are influenced by auto-suggestion stimulated by the heat of the drink. Bitter coffee usually stimulates the appetite while sweet coffee takes the edge off hunger because of the sugar it contains.

Unexpectedly, and contrary to what many people maintain, weak coffee contains a larger quantity of caffeine than stronger. On the other hand it is as well to mention that coffee's euphoric effect is caused by aromatic substances which develop during its preparation, as well as by caffeine. Therefore old or reheated coffee will lack these volatile elements and will taste less pleasant.

Decaffeinated coffee

There is very little caffeine in coffee which has been "decaffeinated", yet if it has been prepared as it should be, it completely preserves the aroma of normal coffee. The caffeine content in a cup of decaffeinated coffee is only 10 milligrams, compared with about 150 milligrams in untreated coffee. Anybody can drink this kind of coffee, even heart patients and those with high blood pressure.

All methods for extracting caffeine from coffee beans employ a solvent, which is nearly always triolein. This solvent is shaken with unroasted coffee beans previously soaked in water. It forms compounds which do not disappear even during roasting; the consequence is that each kilogram of roasted decaffeinated coffee contains two or three milligrams of methylene chloride, which, if not actually harmful, cannot be considered completely healthy. But what matters most to the consumer is the virtual absence of caffeine, which is often erroneously considered responsible for excessive nervous effects.

There are researchers who assert that they would never be great consumers of decaffeinated coffee, because this is nothing but the final resource of the most unrepentant coffee drinker. It would be better to drink a lesser amount of ordinary coffee.

In Italy the consumption of coffee over the last few years reached a peak in the middle of the 1980s (1985) with 2,650 tonnes, particular high points of consumption being in Lombardy, Lazio

and Sicily. The lowest percentage of consumption in relation to the population is in the Marches, Liguria, Umbria, Basilicata and Sardinia.

In the last few years the consumption of decaffeinated coffee in Italy has already reached 400 tonnes per year, while freeze-dried soluble coffee has reached 280 tons.

From the tree to the cup

There are about forty different species of *Coffea*, the coffee tree, the most widespread being *Coffea arabica*, together with *C. robusta*, *C. liberica*, *C. mauritana*, *C. congensis*, *C. stenophylla* and *C. excelsa*. Among these the most widespread and resistant are *C. robusta*, *C. liberica* and *C. arabica*, which have given rise to many varieties in the different regions of production.

The coffee bean is the roasted seed of the coffee tree, a member of the *Rubaciae* family. It almost certainly originated in Ethiopia, but today it has been widely distributed and is cultivated in almost all the tropical regions of Africa, Asia and America.

Coffee cultivation demands a constant climate of between 15° and 25°C (59–77° F) and moist soil in a sloping position sheltered from the wind. The trees are pruned to no more than three metres (10 feet) from the ground, but if left to themselves they can reach a height of eight or nine metres (25–30 feet). This pruning to fairly low heights is done to make harvesting easier.

The coffee tree has oval opposed leaves, scented white flowers arranged in clusters and it produces small round

fruit. The tree bears fruit from three years old for about 30 years; the yield is about 1.5 to 2 kilograms (3½–4½ lb) per year per tree. Brazil produces 400 kilograms per hectare (350 lb per acre) and Colombia 600, but in some warm wet regions the yield can reach 800 to 900 kilograms each year. The fruit contains the seeds, or beans, usually two together, with their opposing faces grooved with a line; they are a little like the hoof print of a miniature wild boar.

Sometimes, particularly with the *arabica* variety, one of the two beans is suppressed by the other, which grows to a round shape.

There are two main methods of extracting the beans from the fruit: dry and wet. With the first the fruit is exposed to the sun. This releases the beans which are then cleaned and sorted according to size and colour.

The wet method involves washing the fruit and stripping it with a special machine; the beans are then fermented and cleaned.

The yield is about 20 kg of coffee per 100 kg of fruit (20 lb per 100 lb).

The coffee bean is quite a delicate product and it can ferment and become acid within six hours of being harvested, particularly when high temperature and humidity make preservation difficult. To prevent this happening a good supply of water must be available, a requirement which must be arranged in advance in some hot countries.

The dry method mentioned earlier results in varieties of coffee which the Brazilians call *corrientes*. When the alternative wet method is used, where the fruit is washed, the resulting coffees are termed *lavados*. These are coffees of great length which are superior to the others.

Nonetheless, the dry system is more widespread in all parts of the world because of its simplicity. The fruits are spread out over *terreiros*, the Brazilian term for the vast courtyards and threshing floors where the coffee fruits are left to dry in the very strong tropical sun. Eventually they become wrinkled, forming a kind of leathery skin. The coffee workers mix and turn the layers of fruits frequently, using shovels, so that the whole surface is exposed to the sun. This operation lasts several days and only an expert's eye can estimate the moment when the beans are sufficiently dry. The coffee beans are then freed from the flesh of the fruit using suitable machinery. But before this operation the beans are passed through a sieve which removes possible impurities and grades them according to size.

The machines for removing the pulp, or to be precise, the shell which has become hard and tough, may be as simple as two round millstones which crush the beans. Commoner today are rotating drums with curved knives mounted inside; these virtually shell the fruits, but they do not remove all the impurities. The next operation therefore involves sieving the beans in several stages to separate the coffee from the other materials such as earth, dust,

small pebbles and pieces of iron (these are removed by magnets).

As already indicated, the method which uses water is more complicated and expensive. The water flows through special channels, conveying the "cherries" through various sieves which remove the shell. The beans are then left in fermentation vats for up to two days, where they lose their sugary layer through continuous washing. Once this operation is over, the beans are spread out directly in the sun or in airy rooms where they are left for three or four days to dry perfectly. These rooms may be artificially heated if the sun is unreliable, as is often the case in the Brazilian highlands for example. The dried beans are then transferred into the *brilladora*, a bronze tube in which the coffee is given the polish needed for grading by the buyers. In the course of these operations appropriate sieves are used to separate the "flat" beans (those found paired in a single fruit) from those that have developed singly, which are generally round and larger; they are sometimes erroneously called "moka".

The industrial coffee-processing plants found where the sacks of coffee are loaded aim more at elegant presentation of the product than at quality, even though some difference between one coffee and another still exists.

The coffee beans are then sent to the large roasting houses where the beans

are loaded into containers which rotate to give them an even roast.

This operation gives the coffee a better balanced aroma. The beans may be roasted light or dark (for example, in Italy, a lighter roast is preferred in the north and a darker one in the south).

The coffee loses about 20 per cent of its weight in the course of processing, but it gains from 15 to 20 per cent in volume. The last stage is for the beans or ground coffee to be packed in bags.

Linked with the roasting process are the "blenders". Nowadays the coffee which is bought in shops or drunk in cafés almost always comes from a single style of production, and the distribution companies are always looking for the best blend that can be achieved by roasting and grinding different qualities of coffee.

The coffee is normally ready to be exported immediately after the process of extracting the beans, but the producers often submit them to polishing, artificial colouring, brushing, and anything else that may improve the external appearance of the beans.

Very occasionally the coffee arrives in Europe (where the greatest consumption is) in the form of the whole fruit. The beans usually arrive here "bare", without their covering.

Until a few years ago, the commercial denominations of coffee took their names from the countries of cultivation

and origin, but today this is no longer so. The brand names which distinguish the individual varieties from each other are chosen almost solely for commercial reasons.

The main qualities of coffee are as follows:

Coffee from Arabia and Africa: Moka, Moka Shortberry, Moka Longberry, coffee from the island of Réunion, coffee from Liberia, from Rio Nuñez, from San Tomè, from Madagascar.

Coffee from the Antilles: Puerto Rico, Guadeloupe, Santo Domingo, Jamaica.

Coffee from North and Central America: Mexico, Mexican Moka, Sierra, Vera Cruz, Guatemala, Salvador, Nicaragua, Honduras, Costa Rica.

Coffee from South America: Brazil, Santos, Venezuela, Colombia, Guiana, Bolivia, Ecuador, Peru.

Coffee from the East Indies: Ceylon, Java.

PRODUCTION AND
HISTORY OF COFFEE

Some notes about production

As far as coffee is concerned the year of production does not follow the solar year, but rather the period from 1 October to 30 September the following year. The timing and size of the harvest also depend on the weather

in the producing country during the year. For example, in 1983–84 Brazilian production was drastically reduced by a prolonged frost in the highlands.

The majority of coffee currently produced is of the *arabica* variety, which single-handedly accounts for 80 per cent of the coffee grown in the world. The different names given to some types or varieties of coffee, such as Sumatra, Moka and Blue Mountain, are misleading, in that they are in fact all *arabica* coffees, but they have been given various names locally and by their producers.

In second place comes coffee of the *robusta* variety, similar to *arabica* except that the trees with umbrella foliage are slightly taller. As the name

suggests, it is strongly resistant to disease, parasites and temperature variation. It is grown in very hot regions in Africa, India and Indonesia. The *liberica* variety comes from Liberia, while the *excelsa* variety (also very similar to *arabica*), is produced in Cameroon, West Africa and Indonesia. It is notable for its ability to survive long periods of drought. In the Ivory Coast the coffee called *stenophylla* exists naturally; curiously, it always has single beans only.

The world annual coffee production today is practically the same as that of tobacco and nearly half that of cotton. Brazil is the largest producer with more than 1,500,000 tonnes; Colombia is in second place with 650,000 tonnes, while Indonesia is third, with over 400,000 tonnes. Somewhat further behind are Mexico, the Ivory Coast, Vietnam, India, Guatemala, Ethiopia, Uganda and Ecuador. Other countries producing good quality coffee are the Philippines, Costa Rica, Kenya, Cameroon, Zaire, El Salvador, Peru and

Venezuela. In total, the overall world production is over 6,100,000 tonnes. Coffee trees thrive in temperate and hot climates, but their greatest enemy is frost which may occur even in tropical climates at certain altitudes. The soil must be rich in nitrogen and potassium, well irrigated and with the certainty of sufficient rainfall. Too much sunlight, such as that provided by the very strong equatorial sun, can be damaging to coffee cultivation, so much so that it is sometimes necessary to protect the trees with overplanting.

A "robust" species

Coffee trees can be susceptible to many diseases – about 20, according to specialists – which attack the roots, stem, leaves or fruit. These include mycosis (fungal diseases), moulds and rust, which are fought by spraying with plant-protection products based on copper sulphate and lime. Today growers have the means to fight these diseases, but in the past they often became epidemic.

But the most dangerous parasite of the coffee tree, causing the greatest concern, is a microscopic fungus of the uredium family which attacks the leaves and ultimately causes the death of the tree. It is not certain, but this fungus probably first appeared on the island of Ceylon (now Sri Lanka) in the second half of the 19th century. From there it spread through southern Asia and Oceania, and then into the African plantations. It has not reached the plantations of Brazil and the other countries of Central and South America. In many of the countries where the fungus spreads and swiftly destroys the harvests, *Coffea arabica* has been replaced by *C. robusta*, which is less subject to the devastation caused by parasites.

Harvesting the berries

It is extremely pleasant to travel in the coffee-growing highlands towards the end of the dry season, when the first rains are brought by the clouds circulating from the sea to the mountains. The hills are all in bloom with little, white, scented flowers combined in clusters forming glomerules at the base of the leaves.

When the flowers fall, the berries mature. In some countries the period of harvesting extends until all the fruits have ripened fully, because the harvesters pass along the rows of trees more than once and pick only the fruits which are ready; the berries which ripen later are checked and picked during later passes.

In Brazil, on the other hand, the harvest takes place in a single operation.

The head of the plantation must decide an "average" point of ripeness, even if some of the fruit is already dry and some of it completely unripe. It is done in this way in Brazil to reduce the cost of harvesting, since a single operation is naturally bound to be much less expensive than several stages of successive harvesting.

Coffeepots

For a long time the history of coffee was identified with that of the coffeepot. The reason is relatively simple: ever since the quality of this black drink was discovered, people have sought to find the best way of making it. In the first place, the fact that the bean of the precious fruit had to be roasted only became apparent after a time. Then, after roasting, the beans must be ground, and here men's imagination could satisfy their whims, following the fashions of the time in which they lived. Grinding was originally carried out with a pestle and mortar. Later on a revolution in the design of coffee grinders took place with the use of metal mills, which with subsequent development took on several different forms. Nearly everyone will recognise the commonest form these pieces of household equipment eventually assumed, even if they have only seen them in antique shops or in old photographs or paintings. This consists of a cube-shaped wooden box with a compartment for the coffee beans, a handle operating a large grinding mill, and a little drawer into which the ground coffee falls.

The first coffee shops were opened in Istanbul at the beginning of the 16th century, and from the drink's earliest appearance the natural way of making it and the one most often followed was to

bring the ground coffee to the boil in water. But this immediately presented a problem: with the grounds in the bottom of the vessel used to boil the coffee, it was very difficult to separate them from the liquid which had now become dark and fragrant. It has been said that the Ethiopians were the first to contrive an ideal coffeepot where the grounds could be removed before drinking the infusion. This is likely to be true because they were probably the first to experiment with making coffee. But then the so-called *ibrik* appeared in

Turkey, perhaps brought there by the Arabs, and it spread throughout the vast Ottoman Empire of the 16th century. This was a container in which water holding the very fine powder obtained by long grinding of the beans was brought to the boil several times, then left until the grounds had settled. The *ibrik* was the forebear of the modern *jisvi*, still used in Turkey and Greece.

When the secret of making porcelain was discovered in Europe at the end of the 17th century (until then the technique had been the monopoly of the Chinese), it was quickly found that porcelain vessels were not satisfactory for preparing coffee. They were tried, but the result was not what was expected. There was something which prevented the coffee grounds expressing all their aroma and taste, when compared with the coffeeobtained with the *ibrik* and the *jisvi*, which were usually made of brass. Next experiments were made with putting the coffee grounds in a bag made of cloth or paper and pouring boiling water over it, very much as is done hastily today with tea bags (a method strongly warned against by the Chinese and Indians, who have an excellent knowledge of tea). Only if the water was made to boil in sophisticated containers of finest silver could a drink be made that was similar, yet not identical, to oriental coffee. But it would have been unreasonable to suppose that everyone would have silver coffeepots at their disposal!

So another method had to be found, using less expensive materials. People experimented with various types of *samovar*, used particularly in eastern Europe (especially Russia) for preparing tea. This was a kind of kettle in which the drink could be kept hot by using an internal metal tube. To make coffee, cloth bags containing the ground coffee were used, on which the hot water slowly dripped when it came to the boil. The *samovar* was heated by simply placing a source of heat under the container. From then on the race was on to improve the coffeepot still further. Even high prelates joined the quest, gluttons for coffee like everyone else. It was the Archbishop of Paris, De Belloy, who made popular a kind of filter coffeepot which evolved, in the German-speaking eastern countries (for example, in Potsdam) into the "invertible" type, the forebear of the Neapolitan pot of today.

Still in Germany, a coffee maker was invented in the early years of the 19th century in which the power of the steam forced boiling water through a central tube and then caused it to fall back onto the ground coffee. Then, when the extinguishable spirit stove was designed in France, people realised that it could also be used in the making of coffee, since this happened quickly as soon as the spirit stove went out. It was this system which almost a century later was used in the construction of the modern coffee machine.

A very similar machine to this was patented in England in 1839.

This was followed by the invention of James Napier – another Briton. He used two containers, one for mixing the water and coffee grounds, and the other (a sort of glass globe) for the coffee itself, which were joined by a syphon tube. This machine was a huge success in Great Britain and many silver-plated examples were made throughout the Victorian period.

A machine was invented in the form of a steam railway locomotive. In Italy

the well-known "trenino di Toselli" was made in earthenware, glazed in red with floral decoration, as the fashion of the period demanded. The "little engine" would be tipped up when the rear "boiler" was full of water. The cover of the spirit stove was raised up and it would fall back and extinguish itself when the weight of the water was transferred to the front part of the engine. Different models of "Toselli's trains" were presented with various decorations; some were made to the specific requirements of customers and they bore the names of women, or coats of arms, or initials of members of the noble families from which customers were descended. In some examples, the sugar bowl took the place of the engine driver's cab (the traditional cabin with an open window). The English satisfied their whims by creating coffee-making locomotives which imitated the robust steam engines designed by the father of

James Napier. At the National Railway Museum in York there is an example of a coffee machine which imitates a locomotive of the Firefly class, designed for service on the Great Western Railway. The arms of the railway company appear on the side of the driver's cab.

By the end of the 19th century the production of locomotive coffee makers and similar playthings gave way to more elegant machines, and creative efforts moved towards the development of more practical objects, better adapted to domestic use.

Coffee as money

When the Ottoman Empire was consolidated in Greece and the Balkans, the Venetians had to give up the trade in goods which they had conducted for so long as virtually a monopoly. Unexpectedly, however, Venice acquired the island of Cyprus, surrendered by the widow of King Giacomo II, the Venetian Caterina Cornaro. Taking control of the island in 1489, Venice turned Famagusta into a naval base and the most powerfully equipped fortress in the whole Mediterranean. After the early years of settlement the first public houses for Venetian sailors to drink in began to appear in the docks and in the corners of the cities of Larnaka and Pafos. These were modelled on those found in Istanbul. Naturally, the favoured drink was still tea, but there was no lack of Turks, who were already preparing steaming cups of coffee.

Venice was already alone among the maritime republics in defending the last commercial (and military) bulwarks of the Orient with all its resources. By now the Spanish and Portuguese were seeking a route to the Indies, which

would provide valuable materials for trade. In doing so they discovered new countries and set up ports along the coasts of Arabia, the very country from which coffee came.

A real crisis for Venice occurred at the end of the 15th century, with the opening of the "route to the Indies" by the exploits of Christopher Columbus. The problem was that coffee and pepper from India cost as much as eighty gold ducats for a quintal (100 kg/220 lb) in Alexandria in Egypt, while in Lisbon American pepper cost only twenty or thirty ducats, in spite of the long voyage round Africa.

The land routes to the Orient were closed to Venice, so the only chance for the future seemed to lie in the importance of coffee, which the Venetians could still buy from the Middle East and Ethiopia. So in the middle of the 16th century Venetian galleys began transporting sacks of coffee beans to the city; these were roasted there and sent to the various parts of Europe. As a result many European merchants reopened their commercial offices which had once flourished, but which had been at least partly transferred to Lisbon on the banks of the Tagus.

In the first half of the 16th century the Portuguese sought to cut off the supplies of coffee and spices which the Arab and Ethiopian merchants were bringing to the warehouses of Venice from Egypt. They occupied the island of Socotra in the ocean off Cape Guardafui on the extreme northern point of Somalia, which controlled the traffic between the Red Sea and the Indian Ocean. They blockaded this route to the Arab vessels that brought the goods to the Venetian merchants. At the same time the Portuguese opened contact with the Amharic Kingdom of Ethiopia, reaching Lake Ascianghi and sending a force of some 400 men as a punitive expedition. Next they established themselves in the famous castles (still extant) built at Gondar. So the whole coast of Eritrea, Somalia and Arabia as far as the straits of Bab el-Mandeb was controlled by Portuguese vessels, which prevented almost all trade with Ethiopia.

The Venetians looked for new ways of obtaining sacks of the precious commodity, which was selling extremely well in Europe. There was the Nile route, which reached Ethiopia by leaving the great river at Khartoum (in those days the only commercial port of Omdurman) and going back up the Blue Nile (called Abai in Ethiopia) as far as Lake Tana, in Amhara, one of the coffee-producing regions. Alternatively one could return up the Atbara and reach the Abyssinian villages.

The search for the legendary Prester John, mythical sovereign of Abyssinia, who was rumoured to possess infinite riches and vast coffee plantations in the highlands, now resulted in an armed Portuguese operation to the Red Sea. This was the end for the Venetian trade. The galleys returned to Alexandria empty and the situation became quite desperate. To the Egyptians Venice proposed digging a navigable canal connecting the Bitter Lakes to the Mediterranean and the Red Sea, but the project was abandoned, so the problem of the Portuguese presence was not solved. This problem became still more pressing: with the Portuguese discovery of Brazil through the exploits of the navigator Pedro Alvarez Cabral, Portugal began the slave trade from west

Africa to nourish the production of coffee (and other foodstuffs) on the highlands of Santos and in the mountains of Espinaçho and Diamantina.

A Portuguese document records that the income of the State in the middle of the 16th century amounted to over 500,000 *cruzados*, of which about 135,000 came from trade in Brazilian coffee. On the other hand, Guinea alone contributed over 10,000 *cruzados* from the slave trade. But the most interesting observation is that sacks of coffee were used as currency, particularly in commercial dealings with Spain. That nation was still the first maritime power and it had conquered the Aztec empire, but coffee could not be grown on the Mexican highlands because of the extreme range of temperature and the shortage of rain. So, the precious beans became actual money.

Faced by the incredible riches being generated by the slave trade, which served to supply labour for the plantations (cotton and sugar cane as well as coffee), even Spain had to descend into the field to avoid being overwhelmed by the success of its eternal adversaries. Catalan and Andalucian ships began to cross the Atlantic Ocean with their holds overflowing with thousands of unfortunates seized from their villages in the Gulf of Guinea, the Congo and Angola, and returned to Spain laden with valuable sacks of coffee.

The Venetians reopened their houses of "Contratación" ("counterattack") in Seville and Malaga. At that time merchants all over Europe called the slave ships by the same name as the Portuguese themselves used, *tumbeiros*, meaning coffins. This was an era when a black man was exchanged for three sacks of Brazilian coffee at the fort of Mina – the fort "Saint George of the Mine" on the Gold Coast.

The production of coffee and the planting of its trees led to economic and political gambles like those in the oil business today. In 1690 a party of Dutch sailors disembarked at Moka, in the Yemen, to capture some little trees. The result was the spread of coffee to Java and Sumatra, in the Indian Ocean. In 1723 a Dutch official was sent to Martinique, a French colony, to plant coffee there. Despite his ship being attacked by pirates, he succeeded in his objective.

The Portuguese quickly began to plant coffee in their possession in Brazil, in the region of Santos and in the highlands behind this ancient settlement The first importers of roasted beans were Dorothy Johnson of Boston, in 1670, and William Penn, in 1683, in the country which was not yet called the United States. That would be the name of the federation formed of the 13 colonies which rebelled against the British: New Hampshire, Massachusetts, Rhode Island, Connecticut, New York, New Jersey, Delaware, Pennsylvania, Maryland, Virginia, the two Carolinas and Georgia. It was natural that well-off American families should still follow the fashions of London, although the times of separation from the Crown were maturing. At that time they used coffeepots of silver or silver plate. Later, North America began to fill with immigrants who arrived from Poland, Russia, Italy and so on, and they would boil the ground coffee in the

typical jugs of eastern and southern
Europe, of Ottoman or Arabic ances-
try. From this use, notably through the
influx of immigrants into Pennsylvania, came the famous cowboys' billycan celebrated in so many Westerns: a
coffeepot which could define the word
"emergency", which served anyone
who had to prepare good coffee in the
morning on the burning embers left

over from last night's fire at the camp.
In 1838 the first American patent for a
replacement for the cowboy billycan
was granted to an Italian immigrant in
Pennsylvania, called Bencini. This
preserved the aroma of the roasted
ground beans better.

The French, the Germans and the
English all sought to devise new tech-
niques for making better coffee, but
they only rarely achieved a result comparable with a little cup of steaming

coffee prepared in Naples at the time of the last Bourbons.

It was not essential to own a machine "with a piston" for pushing hot water through the ground coffee, or one with a little pump which sucked in the water when the handle of the coffeepot itself was operated, or the complicated Portuguese system which needed two containers, one of china and the other

of brass. At home the "Neapolitana" was normally used, while bars and cafés had traditional espresso machines, the most famous being the "Pavoni".

Then came the Moka espresso machine and the preparation of coffee became even simpler. The secret of making good coffee with the Moka is to lower the flame when the first drops appear in the upper container and to raise it again when at least three quarters of the liquid has filled it.

Coffee conquers the world

Perhaps the knowledge of the properties of coffee had its origins about 1,000 years ago, when some Ethiopian shepherds discovered that the sheep and goats which fed on this tree and its fruits became insomniac and irritable. Probably, the Ethiopian shepherds reported the event to the monks of the many Coptic monasteries there. The monks would have investigated and prepared a stimulating infusion. But recent researches in the field have established that the tree called *Coffea arabica* is originally from the Yemen, the Asian land separated by the strait of Bab el-Mandeb from Abyssinia.

Arabs, Ethiopians, Sudanese and the Turks exploited the discovery. There were coffee shops at Medina in Arabia in the 16th century, while the coffeepot was already known in Istanbul in 1511. The Turkish ambassador at the court of the Sun King, Louis XIV of France, gave the sovereign some coffee trees for his gardens, while in Venice the first "coffee house" was opened in the Piazza San Marco in 1683.

Brillat-Savarin, the French physiologist and gastronome, held that a Turkish prince called Suliman Aga introduced the custom of drinking coffee among the Parisian aristocracy more or less in the mid-17th century, and that an American had acquired the trees in

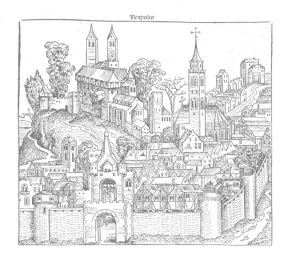

Neapolis

1670. "Immediately afterwards", he added, "the first café opened in Rue Saint André des Arcs, decorated with mirrors and little marble tables, much as are seen today." Brillat-Savarin wrote this in the second half of the 18th century, and it therefore refers to information obtained from others.

One thing is certain: coffee was quickly considered an item of luxury and, as such, it was taxed and the subject of monopoly. In Genoa in 1683 the Rulers of the Great Council forbade the use of coffee, particularly because it was in competition with brandy, a product which was already heavily taxed. But very quickly a coffee monopoly was established, and in 1686 it was extended to all the territories subject to the rule of the Republic of Genoa.

According to Arab scholars, the goats who grazed the first coffee berries were those of an Islamic convent in the Yemen. Others believe that the Archangel Gabriel brought the Prophet Mohammed a potion prepared immediately by Allah, black as the Kaaba, the black stone of Mecca; therefore the word "coffee" would be derived from *kaawa* (and in Arabic, the word for "coffee" is *kawa*). Whatever the case, Mohammed would only have started his journeys and sermons after he had drunk a cup of coffee.

However, it appears more likely that the coffee tree originated in Abyssinia; after all, the Abyssinians conquered southern Arabia – the Yemen – in the 6th century.

COFFEE
AND CULTURE

Coffee houses

All Oriental travellers confirm that the use of coffee was common in Arabia at the end of the 16th century. All the same, in 1511 coffee was branded as a devilish drink by the religious authorities of Mecca. At the end of that century the same thing happened in Istanbul where the Great Mufti (the highest religious authorities) banned the drinking of coffee. But the drink quickly passed to the west, probably because of the sea traffic of the Venetian traders who had come across it in the eastern Mediterranean. The first "coffee house" probably opened in Venice in 1683, but it is possible they had already come into use elsewhere (there is a theory that a coffee house had already been opened in Leghorn).

In Paris the Café Procope became the cradle of the Enlightenment. In London the Lloyds Coffee House was

Alessandro Verri   *Pietro Verri*

the headquarters of the most important insurers in the world. In 1764 in Milan the brothers Verri and Cesare Beccaria, founded the philosophical literary review *Il Caffè*. Nevertheless, in *Bacco in Toscana* ("Bacchus in Tuscany", 1865) Francesco Redi defined coffee as a "bitter and wicked" drink.

Drinking by the "intelligentsia"

At the start of the 17th century, "exotic" drinks began to appear in the English and French salons: beer, tea and coffee. The traditions of beer and tea date back some decades earlier, but for coffee this was the century of achievement.

Coffee was always present at elegant meetings and the habit of sipping this hot, black drink became so widespread that premises were devoted to this pleasure. There, men of fashion and society would meet round the steaming cups to discuss politics, literature and the latest plays. About a century later this habit had assumed such importance that it suggested the title for their aggressive magazine to the avant-garde Milanese intellectuals, the Verris and their friends.

Produced by the Accademia de Pugni ("Academy of Fisticuffs") and published in Milan by Pietro and Alessandro Verri, Cesare Beccaria and other intellectuals of the time, *Il Caffè* was printed in Brescia to avoid Austrian censorship (Brescia was part of the Venetian Republic). The publication appeared regularly from June 1764 until May 1766. Its aim was to promote the interests and culture of the people (through public administration and politics), to oppose prejudice and to encourage the birth of a true civic conscience. These intentions were boldly proclaimed in its programme which it

Num. I.

IL CAFFÈ.

Cos' è questo Caffè? E' un foglio di stampa che si pubblicherà ogni dieci giorni. Cosa conterrà questo foglio di stampa? Cose varie, cose disparatissime, cose inedite, cose fatte da diversi autori, cose tutte dirette alla pubblica utilità. Fra breve: ma con quale stile saranno egli no scritti questi fogli? Con ogni stile, che non annoi. E fin a quando fate vui conto di continuare quest'Opera? Insin a tanto che avranno spaccio. Se il Pubblico si determina a leggerli noi continueremo per un anno, e per più ancora, e in fine d'ogni anno dei trentasei fogli se ne farà un tomo di mole discreta; se poi il Pubblico non li legge, la nostra fatica sarebbe inutile, perciò ci fermeremo anche al quarto, anche al terzo foglio di stampa. Qual fine vi ha fatto nascere un sal progetto? Il fine d'una aggradevole occupazione per noi, il fine di far quel bene, che possiamo alla nostra Patria, il fine di spargere delle utili cognizioni fra i nostri Cittadini divertendoli, come già altrove fecero e Steele, e Swift, e Addisson, e Pope, ed altri. Ma perchè chiamate questi fogli il Caffè? Ve lo dirò; ma andiamo a capo.

Un Greco originario di Citera, Isoletta riposta fra la Morea, e Candia, mal soffrendo l'avvilimento, e la schiavitù, in cui i Greci tutti vengon tenuti dacchè gli Ottomani hanno conquistata quella contrada, e conservando un animo antico malgrado l'educazione, e gli esempj, son già tre anni che si risolvette d'abbandonare il suo paese: egli girò per diverse Città commercianti, da noi dette le scale dei Levante; egli vide le coste del Mar Rosso, e molto si trattenne in Mocha, dove cambiò parte delle sue merci in Caffè del più squisito che dare si possa al mondo; indi prese il partito di stabilirsi in Italia, e da Livorno sen venne in Milano, dove son già tre mesi che ha aperta una bottega addobbata con ricchezza ed eleganza sommma. In essa bottega primieramente si beve un Caffè che merita il nome veramente di Caffè; Caffè vero verissimo di Levante, e profumato col legno d'Aloe, che chiunque la prova, quand'anche fosse l'uomo il più grave, l'uomo il più plombeo della terra bisogna che per necessità si rilsvegli, e almeno per una mezz'ora diventi uomo ragionevole. In essa bottega vi sono comodi sedili, vi si respira un'aria sempre tepida, e profumata che consola; la notte è illuminata, cosicchè brilla in ogni parte l'iride negli specchi e ne' cristalli falpsi intorno le pareti, e in mezzo alla bottega; in essa bottega chi vuol leggere trova sempre i fogli di Novelle Politiche, e quei di Colonia, e quei di Sciffusa,

A

63

commended "to the respect for every prince, government or nation". It successfully publicised the thinking of the Illuministi in Italy. But some personalities, such as the writer and critic Giuseppe Baretti from Turin, opposed it and defined it as useless and buffoonlike. The Accademia dei Pugni was dissolved over a disagreement between Pietro Verri and Cesare Beccaria, and *Il Caffè* ceased publication.

The cup of coffee as a digestive or as a drink to finish a meal gained ground particularly in central-southern Italy. In Milan it was still said that a good meal must consist of "tripe or sausages and above all rice with brains and some good beef". But in Naples, in spite of the impression of general misery, the streets and alleys offered spectacular displays of fish, poultry, macaroni and vegetables, and with the influence of the latest Spanish traditions, a warm welcome was given to the black drink which averted sad thoughts and stimulated a better vision of life.

Goethe in his *Italian Journey* wrote "the Neapolitans not only take pleasure in the taste of food ... there are days of universal merrymaking" and he refers to those numerous festivals when they circulate baskets of fish from the gulf and macaroni (meaning any kind of pasta, but in particular

spaghetti), followed by the unfailing "little cup" of coffee. Agreed, the coffee was normally drunk by the rich, but popular pride meant that the people of the alleys enjoyed living like the nobles of the palaces, at least for a day. Poverty and nobility ...

But already, the "best" people went to the "coffee houses" where children of good birth haughtily served little cups filled with the fragrant infusion. There is an elegant example in a drawing by Gaetano Zampini in the Accademia Carrara di Bergamo, where there is a well-born lady ("all charm and vivacity" as the caption says) serving coffee to a count and marquess. These coffee houses had walls covered with shelves with coffeepots and bottles of liqueurs making a fine display. A similar scene appears as an illustration for Carlo Goldoni's comedy *La bottega del caffè* ("The coffee house"), which was published by Edizione Zatta, Venice, in 1789.

Historic cafés

At the time of the French Revolution a cup of coffee cost six soldi in establishments in the Palais Royal quarter; but only five soldi at shops in the less smart areas of Saint-Germain, or the Porte Saint-Antoine, or near the Pont Neuf. Since the conversations in cafés were above all political, it was easy for every Parisian to get up to date with what had happened in the capital and the projects and proposals of the revolutionaries. By buying a drink or two, anyone could linger over a little table for the whole afternoon and discuss the latest events, read and rail against the *Journal de Paris* or the *Journal général de la Cour et de la Cité*, or sing the *Ça ira* (the protest song of the Jacobins, who had held their first meetings at the Caffè Amaury), and commentate in the intervals on the movements of the Stock Exchange.

Patriots, revolutionaries and common citizens discovered in the cafés of Paris a different way of life, encouraged too between 1789 and 1791 by the terrible weather: it rained often, in both spring and summer, and the cafès, with their comfort, saw a growing clientele

fascinated by the new events which the times quickly brought in their wake. As the historian Giacomo De Antonellis wrote, cafés were deeply involved: "the press reported the Revolution and every café had its political position".

The year 1789 brought two new elements: women were allowed into the cafés, from which they had been excluded by ancient tradition and the national militia was founded. The two facts proved vital to the success of the cafés and of the Revolution.

In particular, immense fame came to the Café de Foy, the smartest of the premises in the Palais Royal quarter, once in the Rue Richelieu and then under the portico of a new building overlooking the gardens where the royal family was accustomed to walk. No longer attended by old fogeys with gold-knobbed batons, financiers and generals, the Café de Foy became the great centre of revolutionary agitation. Meetings were improvised there, processions and demonstrations in public squares were organised, and sometimes people sheltered there from the shooting. At the Caffè Zoppi in Faubourg Saint-Germain was the "theatre for the meeting of the children of Liberty". Other famous cafés were the Café du Rendez-vous, the Père-Duchesse, the

Café de l'Echelle, the Café de Bourbon, the Café Gibet, and the Café de Charpentier.

Turning to Italy, one of the most famous and celebrated cafés in Rome was undoubtedly the Caffè Greco. founded in 1760 by a Levantine (hence the name) in the Via dei Condotti, near the Piazza di Spagna in the very heart of the city. Many who became famous stopped at his rooms. In the first half of the 19th century the Russian writer Nikolaj Gogol wrote a large part of the novel *Dead Souls* at a little marble-topped table there. The French writer Stendhal (whose real name was Henri Beyle) was a regular there; he was the author of *Rome, Naples et Florence*, a classic account, and also of *Promenades dans Rome* ("Walks in Rome") which reflected his love for the Eternal City. The German philosopher Arthur Schopenhauer (1788–1860), "pessimist" by nature, here spoke critically of the German culture of his time. Because of this he was driven out from the café by the "Nazarene" painters, a kind of brotherhood of German artists which had made its base at the Caffè Greco. Various musicians frequently met in the rooms, enjoying the spectacle of a Rome that has today disappeared for ever, which spoke to the hearts of those who then frequented it. On various occasions the Caffè Greco was host to the German musician and composer Felix Jacob Mendelssohn, Franz Liszt, and Richard Wagner who was famous even then.

The Caffè Greco was not the only café frequented by well-known names. There was also the Caffè Aragno, opened in 1888. This coffee house was originally established in the old building where Aragno, a dealer in spirits, had his business. It then opened at a new, more appropriate sight in of the Palazzo Vospi (today it is the Caffè Alemagna, not far from the Palazzo Chigi). The old café, with its little marble tables and shining mirrors in the fashion of the period, has since been replaced by a more modern establishment, but it is still sacred to the political and literary life of the capital, almost as it was at the end of the last century.

Armando Ravaglioli, a great expert on Rome who was also secretary general of the Council of the city, wrote that "most memorable in the annals and lively still in the memories of many is the 'third room' of the café, through which so many celebrated national and international personalities passed; it was the meeting place of writers and journalists, of artists and actors. A memorial tablet on the Via delle Convertite recalls the patrons who fell in the First World War".

Also to be mentioned in Rome are the two cafés in the Piazza del Popolo, Rosati and Canova, meeting places for

Salon pour la lecture des journaux étrangers

CAFÈ FLORIAN
à Venise, Grande Place S' Marc.

the artists who gravitate to the area which is thick with art galleries, studios and antique shops (the Via del Babuino and Via del Corso are nearby).

But undoubtedly the oldest café in Italy is Caffè Florian, still flourishing in the Piazza San Marco in Venice. Its primacy is owed to the fact that it was in Venice that the sacks containing the precious coffee beans arrived, transported by the galleys of the Serenissima. The founder of this coffee house was Floriano Francesconi, whose name was always shortened to "Florian" in the Venetian manner. One of the most regular patrons of this café was the English romantic poet George Gordon, Lord Byron, who used to sit in one of the little rooms glittering with mirrors, reading the local newspaper (he spoke Italian perfectly) or discussing literature and politics with the bystanders. More or less at the same time, Café Florian was also patronised by the sculptor Antonio Canova, the highest representative of neoclassical ideals, who divided his free time between the Villa Falier di Asolo and the luminous peace of the magnificent Piazza San Marco. Earlier, Gaspare and Carlo Gozzi had enjoyed unforgettable hours of discussion there. Although very unlike each other, these two brothers were both lively and implacable commentators of political and literary events. Gaspare Gozzi, founder of the *Gazzetta Veneta*, was a shrewd commentator on Venetian affairs. Carlo Gozzi was more conservative and therefore hostile to the new philosophical currents. On the other hand, Caffè Florian was a perfect viewpoint for both of them to observe and study the lifestyle of Venetians. As Casati and Ortona wrote in a lively survey of historic cafés, Carlo turned Caffè Florian "into a platform and fortress in his literary and theatrical battles against Carlo Goldoni who, through observing interesting people in such cafés, was inspired to write his comedy *La bottega del caffè* ('The coffee house')."

In the 1830s the French poet and prose writer Alfred de Musset was madly in love with George Sand (her real name was Aurore Dupin), one of the most eccentric female characters of the time. He came to Venice to forget his problems and was soon attracted by the atmosphere of the Caffè Florian where the cheerful, carefree patrons distracted Musset from his melancholy. His tempestuous love affair with this woman "dressed as a man" had such an impact on him that he became the mouthpiece for the anguish of his time, that state of mind defined as the "sickness of the century" which caused an individual to be overcome by inexplicable sadness and melancholy.

Meanwhile, Caffè Fiorio in Turin was becoming increasingly famous as the centre for the agitated political life of exiles and nationalists from all over Italy. (Its present address is 8 Via Po; that is, right in the heart of the city.) Santorre di Santarosa, captain of the grenadiers, used to spend time there, haranguing the other patrons with excited speeches. Later he was killed by the Turks at Sfacteria, bravely fighting for Greek independence. Among the regulars at Caffè Fiorio were Massimo d'Azeglio, man of letters, painter and politician, who became prime minister of Sardinia; and Camillo Benso, count Cavour, the main force behind the Unification of Italy. The two men would spend hours discussing the possibilities of a union between the many independent Italian states, while downing numerous cups of black coffee.

The Caffè della Cecchina in Milan was another hub of political activity, favoured by Cavour's followers.

Giuseppe Mazzini's more revolutionary men preferred to meet at the Caffè della Peppina.

But the "moral capitals" of Turin and Milan were not the only cities with coffee houses attracting artists, writers and politicians. The Caffè Pedrocchi in Padua, for instance, designed by the Venetian architect Giuseppe Jappelli, opened in 1830 near the university. (It is at the entrance to the piazzetta of the same name, not far from Cavour's monument.) It was named after its founder Antonio Pedrocchi, whose heir Domenico left it to the municipality of the Veneto town in 1891. While excavating to build the foundations, ruins of a Roman forum were discovered, now displayed at the Museo Civico.

Unusually, this famous coffee house was divided into separate rooms for different types of visitor. The furniture, still there today, was designed by the architect himself. For a long time the café had no doors at the front, because it remained open all day and all night. Patriots, students and writers gathered there, and on 8 February 1848 there was a "historic" fight between Austrian gendarmes and Irredentist students. There is a ballroom on the top floor and next to it the Rotunda Room decorated with fine paintings.

There were also several coffee houses in Florence, where intellectuals and supporters of the progressive movement in literature and art would meet. One of these was Caffè del Giubbe Rosse (the present entrance is in the Piazza della Repubblica), which has always been one of the most active cultural centres in Florence, and indeed Tuscany. It was the meeting place for painters such as Ottone Rosai, journalists such as Arturo Loria who worked for the main national papers, and poets such as Eugenio Montale and Mario Luzi, to name just a few and whose photographs exist. Another regular was the "cursed poet" Dino Campana who came to the Giubbe Rosse to sell his books of "strange" poems; they were not very popular at the time, but his *Canti Orfici* are respected today.

At the beginning of the 20th century, when Florence was the centre of Italian culture and a reference point for European culture, the Caffè delle Giubbe was to some extent the cradle of the new movement in literature. For instance, it was here that the Milanese Futurists came to debate with the Florentines. Here too *Lacerba* was conceived, a magazine of literature and art founded by Giovanni Papini and Ardengo Soffici. The Caffè delle Giubbe Rosse also boasted eminent visitors such as André Gide and Vladimir Lenin.

There was another famous Florentine coffee house which unfortunately no longer exists: the Caffè Michelangiolo in the Via Larga (today the Via Cavour). Some people described it as more important than a university fine art department, while the former mayor Piero Bargellini wrote a book about its regulars, published by Vallecchi. It was here that the "parliament of the new government of the arts was set up ... here that the high court of art criticism was held". It was more than just a coffee house, it was the general headquarters of painters, and it was the seat of the Macchiaioli painters who foreshadowed the Impressionists. Crossing the threshold of this café was enough to indicate support for the movement.

Bargellini wrote: "Not a page of the political, literary, or artistic history of the 19th century could be written without mentioning the name of a coffee house. Originally, in dark premises, run by Turks in turbans or Greeks, smoky and mysterious like alchemists' laboratories, filled with sacks covered in cabalistic signs, a few rare consumers of the wicked, bitter, a drink gathered. But in the course of a century these dark coffee houses became as important as political and academic clubs. Replacing the soporific chocolate drink favoured by aristocrats which was so popular in 18th-century salons, coffee became the preferred stimulant of liberal agitators; so much so that if political movements had distinctive tastes, then the reactionaries would drink chocolate and the revolutionaries coffee."

Photographs exist of other historic coffee houses in Florence: for example, the Caffè delle Colonnine near the Loggia degli Alberti, at the corner of Borgo Santa Croce; and the Caffe dell'Indiano, at the end of the Cascine park with a beautiful view across the Arno.

There are also photographs of the writers and artists who patronised the famous Caffè Giannessi di Viareggio. These faded images of the period show the poet Giuseppe Ungaretti, the author and literary critic Giuseppe Prezzolini, the journalist Enrico Pea of Lucca and the painter and writer Lorenzo Viani from Viareggio.

Among the regulars at these Tuscan coffee houses were other well-known names including the Florentine journalist Aldo Palazzeschi, the Florentine literary critic Emilio Cecchi, the Sienese journalist Federigo Tozzi and Giosuè Carducci, the national poet of modern Italy who was also a character of the coffee houses of Bologna and the Romagna. All were avid consumers of the black beverage so disapproved of by the Arezzo-born Francesco Redi.

Of the famous coffee houses in Naples, the Gambrinus became the heart of the city and the place where its intellectuals gathered, as Giovanni Artieri recalled: "Here literary movements and society are shaped and the burning issues of freedom are discussed". Of course, since the participants were Neapolitans, the tone of the debates was always a mixture of tragedy and comedy.

The Gambrinus was the meeting place of the Neapolitan Novecentisti, followers of avant-garde literary movements of the period. Among them were Massimo Bontempelli and Curzio Malaparte. The group included many other famous people in a Naples that was emerging as a city full of cultural interests and anxieties which in turn "were developed and debated" in these coffee houses. There was Cipriano Marinelli who wrote for a local literary review; Antonio Guerriero who was a literary critic and a harsh critic of customs of the time; Gino Caprioli, pale and rotund like an 18th-century abbot, Antonio Pepe; and many others.

Quite inexplicably the Gambrinus has disappeared today, as have other famous Neapolitan coffee houses like the Testa d'Oro, the Caffè d'Italia, the Croce di Malta in Santa Brigida and the Aceniello at the Porta San Gennaro. The Gambrinus had rooms with large mirrors and panels painted by the most important painters of the region, as well as silent "reading rooms". But its most striking feature was the omnipresent aroma of roasted coffee. The rooms of the Gambrinus were the pagan temple of the arts and literature, "the precious foundry where the best of the city was cast", and the platform for the most avant-garde intellectuals of the city. Edoardo Scarfoglio, a colourful poet and journalist, and his wife Matilde Serao, journalist, columnist and co-founder of the *Mattino di Napoli*, made it their second home.

After the Unification of Italy, artists and writers from the former Bourbon provinces were also attracted to this coffee house and the people who patronised it. The dignified pride of a people thwarted by fate was born in these rooms; and the most avant-garde minds of the south gathered strength from the example of novelists like Giovanni Verga, Luigi Capuana, Federico De Roberto, Giuseppe Antonio Borgese; painters like Francesco Paolo Michetti and Filippo Palizzi; politicians like Francesco Saverio Nitti and Antonio Salandra; famous singers like Enrico Caruso; and, last but not least, "genuineNeapolitans" like Salvatore di Giacomo and Gabriele d'Annunzio, followed by hosts of admirers.

Even today, cafés are still used as

meeting places where people engage in lively debates, but sadly the subject of these discussions is usually sport. They are meeting places where football fanatics gather to discuss the object of their passion, supported by the aroma of ground coffee.

Coffee and art

In collections of prints and engravings of the 19th century there are many works of art depicting Eastern coffee houses. These often show distinguished gentlemen dressed in the Oriental manner sipping their coffee in little town squares, or on some Greek island, or on the banks of the Bosporus.

There are also many paintings by famous artists showing people drinking coffee or portraying the interiors of coffee houses or French pavement cafés, in which the characteristic cast iron tables with marble-tops are easily recognised.

One example that may be defined as "classic" is Vincent Van Gogh's famous

painting *Pavement café in the Piazza del Forum*. It shows a yellow wall, two rows of tables, a customer seated at the corner, and a waiter wearing a long white apron. From the star-studded sky above comes an intense transparent light, making it a typical French night scene. Van Gogh was celebrated for his

café scenes, like that of the Café du Tambourin in the Rijksmuseum at Otterlo, showing a melancholy lady sitting at a table; or *Café at Night* in the New Haven Museum, where customers are sitting in the corner while the light falls on the central billiard table. Many of his still-lifes contain various coffeepots, as can be seen in the Barnes Foundation's De Chabannes collection.

Toulouse-Lautrec painted several café pictures, including *Monsieur Boileau in the Café*, now in the Cleveland Museum of Art, with the subject sitting at one table and more tables and customers in the background. Then

there is the famous *Moulin de la Galette* with cups and saucers in the foreground (the painting is in the Art Institute in Chicago), as well as the paintings inside the Moulin Rouge. Monet and Degas both painted various café scenes, as did the Italians Fattori, Zandomenegh and other painters of the Tuscan Macchiaioli group. The atmosphere of cafés, especially the "café concert" where there was also music and dancing, was a popular theme with painters: one has only to think of Chocolat, Morelle Lender, Cha-U-Kao, Jane Avril, and *La Gouloue* painted by

Toulouse-Lautrec. The café had become a place of entertainment.

Fortune-telling with coffee grounds

Ever since the dawn of the enjoyment of coffee in Turkey, and especially in Istanbul, there have been people who find coffee, or rather coffee grounds, a valuable tool for seeing the future. There are still people in the countries of the eastern Mediterranean who are credited

with reading the future events of the
current year, or even for a longer period,
from the way the coffee grounds are
arranged at the bottom of a *jisvi* or a
coffee cup. (In these countries the coffee
cup will have no handle, because, as the
Arabs say, the cup must transfer the heat
of the restorative drink to the hand of
the person drinking it.) Arabs and Turks
in particular like to read the omens relat-
ing to business or love affairs. Does an
enterprising Mahommedan want to
acquire a cargo and trade with an
Aegean island? Will this commercial
deal be successful? The coffee grounds
will tell. Will the beloved daughter of an
elderly shopkeeper in Galata submit to
the demands of her lover? Again, the
coffee grounds will tell.

It should be remembered that these
attempts at divination did not come into

existence with the arrival of coffee in the Levant. There were already many interpreters of dreams, of plumes of smoke, of the flight of birds, of the fall of the dice and of the arrangement of playing cards.

Even in the cynical times of Western society today, there are people who believe they can interpret the future by reading the coffee grounds! Of course, for reading the grounds, the coffee has to be made using the Turkish method.

The sceptical, on the other hand, prefer to use old coffee grounds as fertilizer for the flowers in pots which make such a fine display on terraces and windowsills.

RECIPES

Variations on Coffee

The classic cup of coffee can be flavoured by adding a little lemon zest or a pinch of cocoa powder. To sweeten it, honey may be used instead of sugar; as well as being healthier it gives it a distinctive flavour.

In summer an excellent drink can be made by shaking coffee with a few small ice cubes until they are all melted, then flavouring it with a few mint leaves.

Drowned Coffee

Ingredients: 4 small cups coffee; 2 small glasses Scotch whisky; 100 g ice cream.

Prepare the coffee in the usual way. Pour half a glass of the Scotch whisky into each cup and then add a generous spoonful of ice cream (vanilla, orange or lemon-flavoured as preferred).

Coffee Bavarois

Ingredients: 6 egg yolks; 200 g caster sugar; 250 g milk; 100 g espresso coffee; 30 g gelatine; 500 g single cream; 1 small glass coffee cream.
Beat the egg yolks with the sugar until the mixture becomes creamy. Then add the milk and the coffee, previously heated and left to cool. Soften the gelatine in lukewarm water and add to the mixture. Put all this mixture on a moderate flame and heat without boiling. Allow to cool down. Whip the cream and add to the mixture. Pour into a mould moistened with the coffee cream. Leave to cool in the fridge for 3 to 4 hours.

Coffee Biscuits

Ingredients: 350 g butter; 750 g caster sugar; 3 eggs; 50 g coffee paste; 750 g white flour, Type 0; 30 g dried yeast; 200 g sultanas.

Beat the butter and the sugar to form a foamy, creamy mixture. Add the eggs and the coffee paste and stir until smooth. Add the sifted flour and yeast. Add the sultanas. Pour the resulting mixture into a pastry bag with a conical nozzle and form small biscuits on a baking sheet. Flatten the biscuits with a spatula, then coat them with beaten egg yolk and sprinkle caster sugar over the top. Bake for 15 minutes in the oven at a temperature of 200° C (400° F).

Coffee and Chocolate Roll

Ingredients: 250 g chocolate; 100 g roasted almonds; 4 eggs; 75 g unsalted butter; 250 g caster sugar; 20 g instant coffee.

Grate the chocolate. Chop the almonds. Separate the egg yolks and whites. Melt the butter over a flame and beat until foaming, then add the sugar, the egg yolks, the coffee, the almonds and the grated chocolate. Whip the egg whites lightly and fold them carefully into the mixture. Lightly grease a cake tin with the butter, pour in the mixture and put in the fridge to set for at least 2½ hours.

Coffee Toffees

Ingredients: A few tablespoons corn oil; 500 g caster sugar; 400 g single cream; 250 g honey; 50 g unsalted butter; 100 ml very strong coffee.

A container divided into small compartments is needed, such as a metal ice cube tray. There will be as many toffees as there are sections. Lightly coat each individual mould with vegetable oil. Heat all the ingredients together except for the coffee and stir until the mixture has a paste-like consistency. Only then add the strong coffee. Stir well while still hot and pour the mixture into the moulds. Leave to cool thoroughly before removing the toffees from the moulds, using a knife if necessary. Wrap the toffees in coloured paper.

Three-colour Cassata

Ingredients: 200 g sponge cake; 200 g vanilla ice cream; 200 g pistachio ice cream; 200 g raspberry ice cream; 200 g mascarpone; 2 tablespoons finely ground coffee.

Cut the sponge cake in two horizontally. Take a cake tin and put one of the two halves in it. On top of it spread a layer of the vanilla ice cream, followed by a layer of the pistachio ice cream. Cover with the other half of the sponge cake and coat it with the raspberry ice cream. Smooth the surface with a spatula and put in the freezer for at least an hour. Mix the mascarpone with the ground coffee to form a soft, creamy mixture. Put this mixture in an icing syringe with a fluted nozzle. Tip out the cassata onto a serving dish and decorate the top and sides with rosettes of the coffee-flavoured mascarpone.

Coffee Cream

Ingredients: 8 eggs; 50 g potato flour; 350 g caster sugar; 5 g pectin (syrup or water-soluble powder); a small sachet of vanilla sugar; 500 ml thin single cream; 500 ml full cream milk; 50 g instant coffee.

Separate the egg yolks and whites. Mix the potato flour with the egg yolks. Beat the egg whites until stiff and add about half the sugar and all the pectin and the vanilla sugar, stirring very gently. Boil the other half of the sugar with the cream and the milk; then dissolve the instant coffee in this mixture. Cook the mixture until it thickens (this can take quite a while). Only then remove it from the heat. Add the beaten egg whites. Allow the coffee cream to cool to room temperature before serving.

Mascarpone Cream

Ingredients: 2 eggs; 4 tablespoons caster sugar; 200 g mascarpone; 1 small glass Jamaica rum, a handful roasted coffee beans for decoration.

Separate the eggs. Put the egg yolks in a bowl, add the sugar and beat until the mixture is foamy. Mix the mascarpone and the rum together, stirring thoroughly but gently to obtain a smooth mixture, and add to the first mixture. Beat the egg whites until stiff and add them to the mixture. Pour it into four ramekins, decorating them with the coffee beans. Put the ramekins in the fridge until they are served.

Coffee-flavoured Crème Patissière

Ingredients: 4 egg yolks; 150 g caster sugar; 30 g white flour; 500 g skimmed milk; 100 ml strong coffee.
Beat the egg yolks with the sugar until creamy and foamy. Add the flour, the milk and the strong coffee.

Put over a moderate heat, stirring very gently with a wooden spoon to make sure that the mixture does not stick to the bottom of the pan. Do not let it come to the boil. The cream is ready as soon as the mixture begins to coat the spoon. Pour it into a suitable or dish and serve straight away.

Coffee and Juniper Pudding

Ingredients: 200 g butter; 300 g caster sugar; 3 eggs; 5 juniper berries; 150 g chopped roasted almonds; small pinch of salt; 400 g white flour; 10 g yeast; 50 coffee beans, finely ground; 100 g sultanas, soaked in warm water.

Mix half the butter with all the sugar and add the eggs. Melt the remaining other of the butter and flavour it with the finely crushed juniper berries and chopped almonds. Add the salt. Mix with the sifted flour and yeast and the finely ground coffee beans. Combine the two mixtures, then sprinkle with the drained sultanas and stir carefully. Pour the resulting mixture into an oiled flan tin and bake in a hot oven at 180° C (350° F) for at least 45 minutes. Serve hot or cold.

Strawberry and Coffee Pudding

Ingredients: 2 eggs; 50 g butter; 400 ml milk; 3 tablespoons caster sugar; 2 tablespoons white flour; ½ small glass brandy; 1 sachet vanilla sugar;

24 Savoy biscuits; 250 g fresh cream;
20 wild strawberries or small garden
strawberries; 2 small cups coffee.
Separate the eggs. Whisk the egg yolks
and add the butter. Stir in the milk, the
coffee, the sugar and the flour. Pour in
the brandy drop by drop while stirring
the mixture. Beat the egg whites until
stiff and fold gently into the mixture,
together with the vanilla sugar. Line the
mould with the Savoy biscuits and add
the mixture. Cook in the oven at 170° C
(340° F) for an hour. Leave to cool, then
garnish with the cream and strawberries.

Meringue and Coffee Pudding

Ingredients: 4 meringues; 250 g single
cream; 50 g icing sugar; 50 ml strong
coffee, cold; 3 egg yolks; 125 g caster
sugar; 50 g egg marsala.
Crumble the meringues into ramekins.
Beat the single cream with the icing
sugar and add the cold strong coffee.
Prepare a zabaglione by mixing the egg
yolks, the sugar and the egg marsala;
cook over a moderate heat and bring
gently to the boil, then leave to cool.
Pour a spoonful of the beaten coffee
cream over the crumbled meringues in

the ramekins and add the zabaglione on top. Leave the pudding in the fridge for several hours before serving.

Ricotta and Coffee Pudding

Ingredients: 4 eggs; 150 g unsalted butter; 150 g icing sugar; ½ small glass brandy; 500 g ricotta; 1 packet Pavesino biscuits; 4 small cups strong coffee (hot); 150 g plain chocolate.

Separate the eggs. Beat the egg yolks and add the softened butter. Stir well. Mix the icing sugar, the brandy and the ricotta. Beat the egg whites and fold in with a spoon. Soak the biscuits in the hot coffee and line a deep cake tin with them. Pour in half the mixture and freeze. Grate the chocolate onto the other half of the mixture and stir it in gently. Pour onto the first half and freeze until hard. Tip out onto a serving dish and serve.

Coffee Flan

Ingredients: 6 eggs; 300 g caster sugar; 250 g strong coffee; 50 g coffee cream.
Separate the eggs. Whisk the egg whites till stiff, then carefully fold in 200 g of the sugar and all the egg yolks, making sure everything is well mixed. Add the strong coffee and the coffee cream. Heat the remaining sugar in a saucepan until caramelised and pour round the inside of a lightly greased mould. When hard pour the prepared cream into it. Cook in a bain marie until set. Turn out and serve hot.

Coffee Ice Cream

Ingredients: 250 ml milk; 10 g instant coffee; 250 ml single cream; vanilla essence; 4 eggs; 150 g caster sugar.
Pour the milk and the instant coffee into a saucepan and bring to the boil. Remove from the heat and add the cream and the vanilla essence. Allow to cool.

Separate the eggs. In a second saucepan whisk together the egg yolks and the sugar. Add the milk, coffee and cream mixture and combine. Stir carefully with a small wooden spoon. Put the saucepan on a moderate flame while stirring very gently, but do not bring it to the boil. Let the mixture thicken, then pour into a bowl. Allow to cool down while still stirring gently.

When cool, put the mixture in the ice-cream machine to thicken it. When it is ready put the ice cream in the freezer to harden. It must be stored at a temperature of between -14° and -16° C (3° to 7° F).

Coffee Sauce

*Ingredients: 1 tablespoon fat;
1 mushroom; 2 carrots; 2 cloves garlic;
1 teaspoon cumin; 2 tablespoons
almonds; 1 tablespoon peanuts;
1 teaspoon powdered cinnamon;
2 cloves; 2 hot red chilli peppers, finely
crumbled; 60 g finely ground coffee
beans; 1 glass warm vegetable stock;
1 tablespoon caster sugar.*
Melt the fat in a saucepan. Finely chop the mushroom, the carrots and the garlic. Mix together and add to the pan.

Add the cumin, the almonds, the peanuts, the cinnamon, the cloves and the chilli peppers, crumbled as finely as possible. Mix gently together on a moderate heat, then sprinkle the finely ground coffee on top. Remove the saucepan temporarily from the heat, and quickly stir in the stock. When the ingredients have been well combined sprinkle on the sugar and put back on a moderate heat. Pour the resulting mixture into a sauceboat and serve immediately.

Coffee Semifreddo

Ingredients: 250 ml milk; 75 g caster sugar; 2 egg yolks; 30 g white flour; 1 teaspoon instant coffee; 1 tablespoon rum; 2 egg whites; 100 g icing sugar; juice from ½ a small lemon; 500 g whipped cream; 1 handful roasted coffee beans.

Mix together the milk, the sugar, the egg yolks, the white flour, the instant coffee and the rum. Put on a low heat and stir until thickened, thus making crème patissière. Remove from the flame and allow to cool down. Whisk the egg whites, combine with the icing sugar, and the lemon juice to make a meringue mixture. Then put the crème patissière in a bowl and add the meringue mixture very gently to it. Reserving a little of the whipped cream to garnish, add the rest of it to the mixture, stirring very carefully from bottom to top. Pour into small moulds and leave in the fridge for at least six hours. Before serving, garnish the semifreddo with the coffee beans and curls of whipped cream.

Tiramisù

Ingredients: 4 egg yolks; 150 g caster sugar; 4 teaspoons dry marsala; 250 g mascarpone; 250 g single cream; 2 dozen Savoy biscuits; 6 small cups strong coffee (cold); 2 tablespoons powdered plain chocolate; a little grated plain chocolate for decoration.
Whip the egg yolks, the sugar and the marsala together and cook gently in a bain-marie to make zabaglione. Next combine the zabaglione with the

mascarpone and the cream, which must be as fresh as possible. Soak the Savoy biscuits in the strong coffee. Spread one third of the cream mixture in a rectangular baking tin, arrange half the biscuits over it, and sprinkle with the powdered bitter chocolate. Repeat with another layer of cream and the rest of the Savoy biscuits. Cover the whole with the remaining cream mixture. Cool in the fridge for about 3 hours and serve cold. Decorate with shavings of grated plain chocolate.

Ligurian Coffee Tart

Ingredients: 4 eggs; 200 g caster sugar; 250 g white flour; 200 g softened butter; 200 g chopped almonds; 30 g potato flour; 60 g coffee liqueur.

Whisk the eggs and stir in the sugar. Ingredient by ingredient, stir in the flour, about half the butter and all the chopped almonds. Gently stir all the ingredients together into a soft paste and then add the potato flour. Next add the coffee liqueur in a thin stream while gently stirring. Meanwhile grease a cake tin with the remaining butter, pour the mixture into it, and bake in a moderate oven at about 170°C (340°F) for an hour. Serve hot.

Coffee Tart with Cinnamon and Vanilla

Ingredients: ½ litre milk; 150 g strong coffee; 400 g white flour; 300 g caster sugar; 100 g unsalted butter; 20 g powdered yeast; a pinch of cinnamon; vanilla essence; 3 whole eggs.

Stir the milk and coffee together, then gradually add the flour, making sure that there are no lumps. Add the sugar, the softened butter, the yeast, the cinnamon and a few drops of vanilla essence. It is best to use a small wooden spoon to stir the mixture as gently as possible.

Separate the eggs. Add one egg yolk to the mixture. Whisk the other two and then add them as well. Next, beat the egg whites into stiff peaks and carefully fold into the mixture. Pour into a round cake tin well-greased with butter. Leave it in a warm place for about two hours or a little longer. Then place the cake tin in a moderately hot oven at 160–170° C (320–340° F) for a little over an hour. Serve hot.

Coffee and Cocoa Tart

Ingredients: 200 g caster sugar; 100 g cocoa powder; 300 g flour; 250 ml milk; 2 egg yolks; 1 teaspoon salt; pinch of cinnamon; 50 g coffee paste; 15 g powdered yeast; knob of butter.

Stir together the sugar, cocoa and flour, add the milk, the egg yolks, the salt, the cinnamon and the coffee paste. Mix into a smooth mixture. Add the yeast and stir well. Grease a tin and pour in the mixture. Cook in the oven at about 170° C (340° F) for an hour. Sprinkle with sugar before serving hot.

Black Russian

Ingredients: ice cubes; 3 parts coffee liqueur (such as Tia Maria); 7 parts Russian vodka; .

This cocktail needs a good coffee liqueur to be successful. The Black Russian is usually prepared in an old-fashioned glass. Put the ice cubes in the glass and pour the liquids over them. Stir and serve.

Coffee Elixir

Ingredients: 200 g very finely ground coffee; 1 glass Jamaica rum; 2 litres vodka; a pinch of cinnamon; 750 g caster sugar.

Put the ground coffee in a bowl. Add the rum. Leave to marinate for at least three days, then add the vodka and cinnamon. Separately, prepare a syrup with the sugar and the same amount of water. Mix all the ingredients together and allow to stand for 6 or 7 days in a carefully sealed container. Finally filter and bottle.

Granita of Coffee with Cream

Ingredients: 100 g instant coffee; 150 g caster sugar; 1½ glasses whipped cream.
Boil the coffee and the sugar in half a litre of water. When the mixture starts to boil leave on a low heat for a couple of minutes. Allow to cool down and put it in the freezer, stirring every half hour to break up the ice as it forms. The granita is served in glasses which have been kept cold in the fridge. Put two tablespoons of the whipped cream in the bottom of each glass. Add the granita and cover with the remaining whipped cream.

Café Grog

Ingredients (for 1 person): 1 small cup of very hot coffee; 1 teaspoon caster sugar; pinch of lemon zest; 1 teaspoon brandy or French cognac (hot).
Pour the hot coffee into the grog glasses (i.e. glasses with metal handles). Then add the sugar, the lemon zest and the hot brandy, and set light to it. Serve immediately.

Irish Coffee

Ingredients (for one person): 1 small cup coffee; 1 teaspoon caster sugar; 1 glass whisky; 1 tablespoon thick cream.
Prepare the coffee as usual. The cup into which it will be poured must be slightly larger than the usual cup. Sweeten to taste, but not too much. Add the whisky and gently pour the cream over a teaspoon so that it floats on the top.

Viennese Coffee

Ingredients: ground coffee for four people; 4 teaspoons caster sugar; 4 tablespoons full cream milk; 4 tablespoons whipped cream.
Prepare the coffee as usual. Pour the coffee into each cup and sweeten moderately. Allow to cool. Put the cups in the fridge to chill. Next, pour the cold coffee into glasses or teacups and let each person add a spoonful of milk and another of whipped cream.

Bibliography

A. Brillat-Savarin, *Physiologie du Goût*, Paris 1797.

L. Van Delden, *Le culture du café*, The Hague 1885.

B. Belli, *Il caffè*, Milan 1910.

P. L. Levati, *Vita genovese dal 1699 al 1722*, Genoa 1912.

L. Manetti, *Manuale del droghiere*, Milan 1926.

L. Valerio, *Caffè e derivati*, Milan 1927.

P. Bargellini, *Caffè Michelangiolo*, Florence 1944.

N. Barber, *I signori del Corno d'Oro*, Milan 1974.

A. Petacci, *La cucina della mezzaluna*, Milan 1974.

A. Ravaglioli, *Roma, vedere e capire*, Rome 1980.

A. Zorzi, *Una città, una Repubblica, un Impero*, Milan 1980.

Comitato italiano del Caffè, *Indagine sul mercato del caffè in Italia*, 1984.

T. Mauger, *The Bedouins of Arabia*, Paris 1987.

E. Casati, G. Ortona, *Il caffè*, Bologna 1990.

INDEX

AN ANCIENT TRADITION

Coffee: always a friend 11

What does coffee contain? 16

Caffeine 18

Each to his own coffee 20

Decaffeinated coffee 22

From the tree to the cup 24

PRODUCTION AND HISTORY OF COFFEE

Some notes about production 35

A "robust" species 38

Harvesting the berries 39

Coffeepots 41

Coffee as money 47

Coffee conquers the world 56

COFFEE AND CULTURE

Coffee houses 61

Drinking by the "intelligentsia" 62

Historic cafés .66

Coffee and art 81

Fortune-telling with coffee grounds . .84

RECIPES

Variations on Coffee 89

Drowned Coffee 89

Coffee Bavarois 90

Coffee Biscuits 91

Coffee and Chocolate Roll 91

Coffee Toffees 92

Three-colour Cassata 93

Coffee Cream .94

Mascarpone Cream 94

Coffee-flavoured Crème Patissière . . .95

Coffee and Juniper Pudding 96

Strawberry and coffee pudding 96

Meringue and Coffee Pudding 97

Ricotta and Coffee Pudding 98

Coffee Flan 99

114

Coffee Ice Cream 99

Coffee Sauce .100

Coffee Semifreddo 101

Tiramisù 102

Ligurian Coffee Tart 103

Coffee Tart with
Cinnamon and Vanilla 104

Coffee and Cocoa Tart 105

Black Russian 106

Coffee Elixir .106

Granita of Coffee with Cream 107

Café Grog 107

Irish Coffee .108

Viennese Coffee 108

Bibliography .109

The Connoisseur's Companions

Also in the series:

Chocolate

Delicious and simple-to-make recipes and quirky anecdotes are just a small part of this charming gift book for the chocolate lover.

Whisky

An intriguing account that explains why whisky has become one of the most important drinks in the world. No whisky devotee will want to be without this book.

Olive Oil

Olive oil has become the single most important ingredient in cooking today. Also featuring delicious recipes, this is a useful, concise, easy-to-follow guide.